Original title:
Into the Blue Beyond

Copyright © 2025 Swan Charm
All rights reserved.

Author: Paulina Pähkel
ISBN HARDBACK: 978-9908-1-4756-7
ISBN PAPERBACK: 978-9908-1-4757-4
ISBN EBOOK: 978-9908-1-4758-1

Whispers of Dawn

The sun peeks over the hill,
Soft rays begin to shine.
Birds awaken with a thrill,
Nature stirs, so divine.

Morning dew on grass bright,
Glistening in the light.
A gentle breeze takes flight,
Bringing day from night.

Colors dance in the sky,
Painting clouds with delight.
As the world starts to sigh,
Embracing day so bright.

Footsteps echo in the park,
People laugh and smile.
Children playing till it's dark,
Joy filling every mile.

As the sun begins to set,
Golden hues fill the air.
Ending day, a sweet duet,
Soft whispers everywhere.

Beyond the Indigo Veil

Whispers dance upon the breeze,
Beneath the twilight's gentle tease.
Stars awaken, softly glowing,
In shadows where the night is flowing.

Veils of indigo wrap the sky,
In dreams where secrets softly lie.
The heart begins to gently soar,
With hopes and wishes to explore.

Moonlight weaves through branches bare,
Painting stories in the air.
Where time stands still, and spirits rise,
Beyond the veil, where magic lies.

The Realm of Endless Waters

A mirror vast, of dark and light,
The waters stretch beyond the night.
Each ripple sings a melody,
Of mysteries yet to be free.

Beneath the waves, the shadows play,
In depths where dreams might drift away.
Soft currents guide the wayward heart,
To realms where all things can restart.

Glistening shores with sands like gold,
Awakening tales of old retold.
In every drop, a story spun,
The realm of water, all are one.

Dreams Adrift on Turquoise Tides

Beneath the sun's warm, tender gaze,
Dreams adrift in summer's haze.
Turquoise waves embrace the shore,
With whispers of what came before.

Footprints trace the sandy land,
Where hopes are born and futures planned.
Magic lives in ocean's swell,
In every tide, a tale to tell.

Seagulls soar, their cries are free,
Echoing the soul's decree.
With every break, the heart will rise,
On turquoise tides, we chase the skies.

Secrets of the Sapphire Abyss

Deep within the sapphire sea,
Lies a world of mystery.
Whispers echo through the blue,
With tales of wonders, old yet new.

Creatures glide in graceful arcs,
Guarding secrets, ancient sparks.
In shadows where the light can't reach,
The soul finds depths the heart can teach.

Silence reigns in watery halls,
Where the heart of ocean calls.
In the calm, a universe spins,
In sapphire depths, the journey begins.

Floating Through Celestial Veils

Stars dance softly in the night,
Whispers of dreams take their flight.
Clouds like silk, they gently sway,
Guiding wishes far away.

Moonlight bathes the world in grace,
Time stands still in this vast space.
Hearts entwined in starlit glow,
Finding peace in the ebb and flow.

Galaxies spin in silent song,
Echoing where we all belong.
Above the chaos, still and bright,
Floating through the endless night.

The Vastness of Unseen Realms

Beyond the edge of sight and sound,
Mysteries in shadows abound.
Whispers weave through the hidden air,
In unseen realms, we dare to share.

In the gaps between the stars,
Echoes of time are never far.
Waves of thought like tides roll in,
Revealing worlds where dreams begin.

Truth unfurls in quiet sighs,
In the vastness, the spirit flies.
Hold your breath and take the leap,
Into the realms where wonders sleep.

The Colors of Twilight Depths

Crimson blush of the dying day,
Wraps the sky in soft array.
Indigo whispers through the haze,
As nightfall starts its gentle blaze.

Golden rays weave through the trees,
Kissed by the cool, caressing breeze.
Lavender shadows slowly creep,
Painting dreams that drift and seep.

Silenced echoes of the light,
Merge with the falling velvet night.
In twilight depths, we find our way,
Colors blend, and hearts will stay.

Beneath Vibrant Archives

A tapestry of tales unfolds,
In vibrant archives, secrets hold.
Pages whisper of times long past,
Stories linger, shadows cast.

In each corner, a memory gleams,
History woven through our dreams.
Richly colored threads entwine,
Crafting worlds where hearts align.

Ancient voices softly call,
Beneath the weight of time's great thrall.
Here, in this haven, we will dwell,
In vibrant archives, all is swell.

Whispers of the Azure Horizon

In the morning light, dreams arise,
Softly glowing, beneath wide skies.
Waves of whispers gently call,
Secrets hidden, known by all.

Colors dance on ocean's edge,
Nature's beauty, a vibrant pledge.
Every glance, a fleeting sigh,
Stories woven, the heart's reply.

Clouds drift by, like wishes sent,
In their shadows, time is bent.
Horizon beckons, a sweet embrace,
Infinite journeys, a tangled lace.

Stars ignite as night unfolds,
Timeless tales, their warmth beholds.
Echoes linger in twilight's shade,
Whispers of hope that never fade.

With each heartbeat, dreams take flight,
In the azure, all feels right.
Together we soar, hand in hand,
In this realm, forever we stand.

Echoes from the Celestial Depths

In the stillness, silence hums,
Galaxies dance as stardust drums.
Voices whisper from realms untold,
Ancient stories in the cold.

Nebulas swirl in colors bright,
Painting the canvas of the night.
Each twinkle speaks of journeys far,
Map the paths of every star.

Time is woven like a thread,
Past and future, where dreams are fed.
Echoes linger in cosmic space,
Finding meaning in the chase.

As comets blaze through velvety skies,
They carry hope in their swift rise.
In the dark, a shimmer glows,
Guiding spirits where no one goes.

Listen closely, the universe sighs,
In the dance of light, wisdom lies.
Through the depths, we shall explore,
Echoes guiding us evermore.

Chasing the Crystal Skies

Up above, the wonders play,
Beneath the sun's warm ray.
Clouds as soft as cotton dreams,
Whispers heard in sunlight beams.

Winds of change brush past our faces,
Taking us to far-off places.
Kites of fortune, soaring high,
In the depths of the azure sky.

Through the storms, we find our way,
In every twilight and bright day.
Each horizon holds a tale,
Of adventures where dreams prevail.

As the stars begin to gleam,
We hold tight onto the dream.
Sailing softly through the night,
Chasing shadows, seeking light.

Endless skies, a boundless sea,
In every heart, a wish to be.
Together, let's embrace this flight,
Chasing magic until the light.

Navigating the Wind's Embrace

Gentle breezes, whispers low,
Through the branches, soft they blow.
Guiding us to paths unknown,
In their warmth, we feel at home.

Wings take flight on currents strong,
Nature's rhythm, a soothing song.
Every gust a timeless dance,
Leading hearts into a trance.

Mountains echo with the call,
Through the valleys, wisdom falls.
In the embrace of the airy streams,
We wander freely in our dreams.

With the dawn, new journeys start,
In the wind, we find our heart.
Traveling where the wild winds roam,
In each breeze, we find our home.

So let us rise, let spirits soar,
On the winds, forevermore.
Navigating with grace and ease,
In the dance of nature's breeze.

Reveries Above the Cloudline

In whispers soft, the dreams take flight,
Above the clouds, in silver light.
A canvas stretched, where thoughts reside,
In realms of peace, our hearts confide.

The winds will carry tales untold,
Of journeys bright, of spirits bold.
With every breath, we touch the sky,
In reveries, we learn to fly.

A dance of shadows, light shall play,
In drifted hopes, we find our way.
With wings of faith, we shall ascend,
To where the earthly bonds may end.

Cloud castles rise, as visions gleam,
In twilight's glow, we dare to dream.
With every pulse, the heartbeats race,
In lofty heights, we find our place.

Embrace the calm within the storm,
A mystic bond, a whispered charm.
Above the cloudline, spirits soar,
In endless skies, forevermore.

The Luminous Pathway

Upon the stones, the lanterns glow,
A path unfolds, where dreams may flow.
Each step we take, a story spun,
In golden light, our hearts become.

The shadows dance, in flickering flames,
As hope ignites, we call out names.
With every breath, we pave the way,
To find the dawn in yesterday.

In twilight's hush, the stars align,
Whispers of peace, a sacred sign.
Through garden blooms, the breezes sigh,
The luminous path leads ever high.

With every turn, new worlds arise,
In vibrant hues, beneath vast skies.
The journey's end, just a new start,
For joy resides within the heart.

So walk with me, this path so bright,
Together we'll embrace the light.
With courage found in every stride,
The luminous road, our dreams will guide.

Stars Adrift in Silent Seas

In midnight's grasp, the stars take flight,
Adrift in silence, a wondrous sight.
Their glimmers weave through velvet hues,
A cosmic dance of whispered news.

The waves below, they softly sway,
As cosmic wonders spend the day.
In tranquil realms, where time stands still,
The universe, a heart to fill.

Each twinkling light, a distant dream,
A hint of hope in soft moonbeam.
The ocean's breath, a lullaby,
Beneath the vast, eternal sky.

We sail through nights, where silence reigns,
The stars our guide through joy and pains.
With every glance towards the deep,
We gather thoughts, our souls to keep.

So let us drift on seas of calm,
In starlit nights, we find our balm.
Adrift we are, yet anchored tight,
In celestial love, our boundless flight.

Beneath the Canopy of Dreams

In whispering woods, where shadows blend,
  Beneath the branches, time shall bend.
  The leaves will sing, in breezes sweet,
  A shelter found, where hearts can meet.

  With every rustle, secrets shared,
  In this embrace, we've always cared.
  The colors shift, from dusk to dawn,
  Within this realm, we're never gone.

  A tapestry of light and shade,
  In nature's arms, our fears will fade.
  The twilight glows, a soft caress,
  With every heartbeat, we are blessed.

So linger here, where dreams take root,
In this fertile soil, our hopes bear fruit.
Together we'll weave the stories spun,
  In unity, our souls are one.

Beneath the canopy, dreams will soar,
In every heart, there's so much more.
In whispered thoughts, we'll find our bliss,
  In timeless love, we'll never miss.

Whispers of the Ocean's Embrace

The waves caress the shore gently,
Secrets carried with every tide.
Seagulls dance on the morning breeze,
Nature's song, a tranquil guide.

Shells whisper tales of ancient times,
Stories of love and of loss entwined.
Colors shimmer under the sun,
In this realm, peace we often find.

The salty air invigorates deep,
A soothing balm to restless souls.
Ripples share their quiet dreams,
As the ocean's heart, softly rolls.

Moonlight bathes the sea in silver,
A canvas painted bright and fair.
In its glow, the world feels lighter,
A moment's magic fills the air.

Each splash a memory set afloat,
Echoes of laughter, joy, and pain.
In the depths, our hopes surrender,
To the ocean's wild, sweet refrain.

A Skyward Journey

Beneath the clouds, we spread our wings,
Chasing the horizon's glowing light.
With hearts ablaze, we take to skies,
In search of dreams that soar in flight.

The sun ignites the morning dawn,
A burst of colors, warm and bright.
Birds sing praises to the day,
In freedom's dance, our spirits ignite.

As stars emerge in twilight's glow,
Whispers of wishes fill the night.
Each constellation paints a path,
Guiding lost souls in their plight.

Winds carry tales of distant lands,
Stories woven in twilight's threads.
Adventure calls, we heed the sound,
Our hearts entangled, where dreams are led.

In every journey, a lesson learned,
To trust the skies with all our might.
For in each flight, we find our home,
In the vastness, an endless height.

Echoes of Celestial Dreams

Stars flicker softly in the night,
Whispers of secrets, old and new.
The cosmos hums a gentle tune,
A dance of light, a dream come true.

Galaxies swirl like painter's brush,
Each stroke a dream in flight unfolds.
Nebulas cradle beginnings bright,
In the canvas of the dark, bold.

Nebulae blossom in vibrant hues,
A tapestry woven by cosmic hands.
Hope lingers in the stardust drift,
Our wishes carried to distant lands.

With every twinkle, a story told,
Of wanderers lost in time's embrace.
In the silence, the universe speaks,
Reminding us of our rightful place.

So gaze upon the endless night,
And feel the warmth of dreams ignite.
For within each star lies a promise,
An echo of love and pure delight.

Horizons Awakened

With dawn's first light, the world stirs wide,
Colors blend as day breaks free.
Mountains rise, kissed by golden rays,
In this moment, we're just meant to be.

Fields of green stretch far and wide,
Whispers of nature craft the scene.
Every blade of grass tells a tale,
In the breeze, life's rhythm serene.

Rivers flow with purpose clear,
Carving stories in the earth's warm heart.
Each ripple reflects hopes anew,
As vibrant dreams begin to start.

The sky, a canvas brushed with dreams,
Birds take flight on winds of change.
In their paths, we find our voice,
And step into futures, wide and strange.

Horizons beckon with open arms,
Inviting hearts to voyage far.
In every journey, we discover truth,
As life unfolds beneath the stars.

Truce of Water and Sky

Above the waves, the clouds drift slow,
Whispers of peace in the sun's warm glow.
Blue meets blue in a tranquil embrace,
Harmony found in this vast, open space.

Ripples reflect the colors so bright,
Nature's own canvas, sheer pure delight.
Together they dance, without fear or care,
A bond unbroken, suspended in air.

Fleeting and fleeting, the moments we chase,
In the stillness of time, we find our place.
Tidal waves come, yet they must recede,
Water and sky, both gentle and free.

A Journey Beyond the Fractured Surface

Beneath the waves lies a world unknown,
Mysteries whispered, in soft undertone.
Cracks paint the façade of a vibrant skin,
Yet life thrives deeply, where shadows begin.

Dive through reflections, a realm of the lost,
Seeking the beauty at immeasurable cost.
Each ripple a story, a tale to unfold,
In the heart of the current, the brave and the bold.

The grotesque and the graceful, a juxtaposed dream,
In the dance of the depths, all is not as it seems.
Emerging from darkness, the colors ignite,
A journey continued, into the light.

Celestial Currents and Ocean Breeze

The stars may shimmer with secrets untold,
While moonlight blankets the sea, soft and cold.
Currents intertwine where the heavens align,
A tapestry woven, both sacred and divine.

With every wave lapping on shore with a sigh,
The ocean whispers secrets that never die.
Wind carries tales of faraway lands,
Past shores of wonder, where the heart understands.

Celestial rhythms guide every sail,
In this symphony crafted by nature's own trail.
Listen closely to whispers of the breeze,
As night meets the water beneath the tall trees.

The Enchantment of Distant Shores

Across the horizon where sky meets the sea,
Lie shores of enchantment, where spirits fly free.
A tapestry woven with threads of allure,
Where each grain of sand holds stories secure.

Footprints in twilight lead paths to the past,
Echoes of laughter, where memories last.
The salt in the air sings songs of the deep,
As dreams intertwine with the tides in their sweep.

With brimming horizons, adventurous calls,
Boundless the journey, the heart never stalls.
For in every wave, a new story starts,
At distant shores where the ocean imparts.

Heartbeats Beneath the Surface

In whispers soft, we tread the night,
The moon above, a guiding light.
Our dreams entwine like shadows cast,
In heartbeats deep, the moments last.

A surface calm hides tales untold,
Of rivers deep, of depths of gold.
Each breath we take, a silent plea,
To dive beneath, to truly be.

In echoes lost, our laughter rings,
A melody of hidden things.
The water stirs, our spirits play,
In heartbeats found, we drift away.

A dance of waves, a tranquil sound,
In secret places, love is found.
With every pulse, we bridge the gap,
In heartbeats shared, we close the map.

So here we stand, on edges worn,
In twilight's grasp, a new dawn born.
With love that flows, and hearts unchained,\nIn every beat, forever gained.

Skybound Reveries

Above the world, where dreams ascend,
In azure realms, our hearts will blend.
A canvas vast, the clouds drift by,
In skybound dreams, we learn to fly.

With wishes tossed like stars at night,
We chase the dawn, we grasp the light.
Each thought a feather, light and free,
In reveries of all we could be.

Through cotton clouds and golden rays,
We dance in joy, through endless days.
The sun our guide, the wind our song,
In skybound love, we both belong.

Each moment cherished, time stands still,
As echoes whisper, hearts they fill.
In every glance, a world anew,
In skybound dreams, it's me and you.

So soar with me, through azure seas,
With wings of hope, on gentle breeze.
In timeless flight, let spirits soar,
In skybound realms, forever more.

Valleys of Mist and Wandering Stars

In valleys deep, the mists arise,
Where secrets dwell beneath the skies.
The stars above, they gently shine,
In wandering paths, our hearts entwine.

Through whispers soft, the night is still,
A tranquil peace, a breath, a thrill.
The shadows dance in moonlit glow,
In valleys deep, our spirits flow.

Each step a melody, pure and sweet,
In hidden trails where dreamers meet.
With every turn, a tale to tell,
In misty valleys, all is well.

The stars align in cosmic grace,
Each twinkle beams a warm embrace.
In wandering ways, we seek the truth,
In valleys deep, reclaim our youth.

So take my hand, through fog and light,
We'll chase the dawn, we'll greet the night.
In valleys lost, our truth resides,
With wandering stars, love ever guides.

Between Sail and Sky

With sails unfurled, the wind we chase,
In open seas, we find our place.
Between the waves and azure high,
In harmony, we sail the sky.

The sun dips low, a fiery glow,
As currents pull, we gently flow.
Each moment's breeze, a call to roam,
Between the tides, we find our home.

The stars ignite, a map so clear,
In whispered dreams, your voice I hear.
The ocean's breath, our endless dance,
Between the sail, we take our chance.

With every wave, the world expands,
As time dissolves, we clasp our hands.
In every swell, our hearts align,
Between the sail and sky we shine.

So let us drift, on winds of fate,
With every heartbeat, we create.
In tranquil seas, our spirits fly,
Between the earth, the stars, and sky.

The Tide's Embrace

Whispers of salt in the air,
The ocean sings without a care.
Glistening foam, a white cascade,
Embracing shores in soft charade.

Footprints vanish with each wave,
Secrets held the sea does save.
Moonlight dances, waves collide,
Nature's rhythm, we abide.

In the distance, ships do sail,
Carrying dreams on a gentle trail.
The tide flows in, then pulls away,
A timeless call, where hearts may play.

Waves break softly on the sand,
Caressing every grain so grand.
In the ebb and flow we find,
A tranquil peace, a soothing mind.

Ocean's heartbeat, calm and deep,
In its cradle, secrets keep.
The tide's embrace, a lover's song,
Where we all truly belong.

Moonlight on Wandering Waves

Silver beams on water bright,
Guiding dreams through the night.
Ripples dance, a soft ballet,
Whispers of the sea at play.

Glimmers spark in every crest,
Nature's canvas, at its best.
Waves wander beneath the stars,
A journey free, without bars.

Shores awake with gentle sighs,
Embracing tales of the wise.
Echoes linger, stories told,
In moonlit mirrors, hearts unfold.

The sea hums a lullaby,
Melodies as time slips by.
Each wave carries a secret fate,
Kisses left for those who wait.

As night falls on wandering tides,
Within the waves, the spirit hides.
Moonlight glows, a silver seam,
Guiding us through every dream.

Craving the Infinite

In the vastness we reach high,
Yearning for the endless sky.
Stars like diamonds, bright and bold,
Stories whispered, dreams retold.

A tapestry of night unfolds,
Mysteries in the dark it holds.
The universe sings a song,
In its vastness, we belong.

Boundless journeys, hearts set free,
Exploring depths of the deep sea.
Infinity calls with open arms,
Embracing all its wondrous charms.

Galaxies twirl in cosmic dance,
Giving every soul a chance.
In the quiet, our spirits soar,
Craving more, we seek the core.

With every step, we chase the light,
Finding hope in the endless night.
Craving the infinite above,
A journey guided by pure love.

Skylines of Nostalgia

City lights blink in the dusk,
Memories rise, they feel so just.
Echoes of laughter fill the street,
A fleeting time, a bittersweet.

Skylines tower with silent grace,
Holding stories in every space.
Each building whispers tales of old,
In every corner, dreams unfold.

Familiar faces drift in view,
Moments cherished, tried and true.
Golden sunsets paint the scene,
A canvas where we've always been.

Underneath the starlit skies,
We find the truth in all our lies.
Skylines glow with a gentle hue,
Nostalgia beckons, strong and true.

With every breath, we reminisce,
Longing for a time we miss.
In the skyline, our hearts connect,
A cherished past we must protect.

A Journey through the Cerulean Expanse

Amidst the waves, a whisper calls,
Beneath the sky, the horizon sprawls.
Footprints traced on sandy shores,
Endless blue, where adventure soars.

Seagulls dance on the salty breeze,
Nature's rhythm brings us to our knees.
In every crest, a story we find,
In every depth, the heart unwinds.

Wanderlust fuels the soul's desire,
As the ocean sings like a living choir.
With every tide, we lose and gain,
In the embrace of sea and rain.

Stars above, they guide our quest,
In this expanse, we are truly blessed.
The cerulean vastness knows our name,
With each wave, igniting our flame.

The journey weaves through pulse and tide,
An eternal dance, a soothing ride.
In this world where dreams are cast,
Our spirits soar, forever vast.

Embracing Ocean's Ether

Beneath the moon's soft, silver glow,
The ocean holds secrets only it knows.
Whispers of tales from long ago,
Where time stands still, and currents flow.

Glimmers of light on the darkened sea,
Invite us to join in the wild spree.
With open hearts, we explore anew,
Every wave, a promise, breaking through.

Echoes of laughter dance in the spray,
As we embrace night turning to day.
Each ripple carries a piece of song,
In this ether, we all belong.

The breeze it carries, salt and glee,
Wraps us tightly in its decree.
With open arms and spirits high,
We meld with the ocean, we learn to fly.

Within the depths, our souls unite,
Guided by stars in the blanket of night.
Together, we journey, side by side,
In ocean's embrace, forever we glide.

Reflections on a Celestial Canvas

Above the world, where dreams take flight,
A canvas stretches, vast and bright.
Stars like diamonds, scattered in grace,
Paint the night with their sparkling lace.

Each twinkling light tells a story true,
Of galaxies far, of me and you.
In silence, we ponder our place in time,
As constellations dance, creating rhyme.

The moon hangs low in a velvet sky,
Its glow a balm when we sigh.
Shadows whisper and hearts ignite,
In the reflection of that celestial light.

Every moment captured, a fleeting frame,
In this canvas of life, we're never the same.
Brush strokes of laughter, pain, and love,
Each stroke a blessing from above.

So here we stand, gazing afar,
In wonder of the universe's bizarre.
With each heartbeat, our stories blend,
On this canvas, creation won't end.

Uncharted Waters of the Soul

In the depths where shadows blend,
Lies a realm that has no end.
Waves of thought, they ebb and flow,
Charting paths we long to know.

With every breath, the currents change,
Unfamiliar tides feel so strange.
Yet in this chaos, peace we find,
In the uncharted, hearts unwind.

Drifting through emotions untamed,
In waters murky, truth's proclaimed.
Beneath the surface, treasures gleam,
In solitude, we dare to dream.

The journey is fraught, yet we press on,
Riding waves until the dawn.
With every challenge, we rise, we fall,
In these waters, we learn to call.

And when the storms begin to wane,
The soul finds solace in the rain.
In uncharted realms where we roam,
We uncover ourselves, we find our home.

Ceilings of Water and Sky

Beneath the blue, shadows play,
Reflections dance in the light of day.
Waves whisper secrets to the shore,
An endless journey to explore.

Clouds gather, a canvas of grace,
Mirroring dreams in a tranquil space.
Nature's breath in every sigh,
Where the water meets the sky.

Ripples shimmer, tales unfold,
Of adventures brave and bold.
Skies weep tears of silver rain,
Cleansing the earth, washing pain.

Stars above begin to gleam,
While the moon ignites the stream.
In the stillness, time suspends,
As night descends, the magic blends.

A gentle breeze, the world so wide,
Embracing all as day's tide.
In the harmony of earth and blue,
Ceilings blend, a dream come true.

The Twilight Drift

In twilight's glow, the world transforms,
Golden hues in quiet storms.
As shadows stretch, the light recedes,
Whispers linger among the trees.

A tranquil hush, the day takes flight,
Stars awaken, bidding goodnight.
The horizon blurs in dusky grace,
Wonders hidden in time's embrace.

Gentle sighs of evening air,
Carried dreams without a care.
Softly, the night unveils its heart,
Crafting stories that won't depart.

Moonlight dances on silver streams,
While crickets sing of secret dreams.
In this drift, our souls align,
Bound by the magic of the divine.

As night unfolds its velvet cloak,
A tapestry of thoughts bespoke.
In twilight's arms, we find our way,
An endless night, a new day's sway.

Spheres of Cosmic Flow

In the vastness where stars collide,
Cosmic wonders, a timeless ride.
Galaxies swirl, a dance of light,
Creating worlds in the deep night.

Orbiting dreams in endless flight,
Celestial bodies ignite their might.
Through the cosmos, our spirits soar,
Connected in ways we can't ignore.

From the whispers of a distant sun,
To the pulse of moons that have begun.
Each rotation tells a tale,
Of love and loss in the cosmic veil.

Nebulae bloom in colors bright,
Painting silence with hues of night.
In the vastness, we are all one,
Spheres of flow, beneath the sun.

Together we drift on starlit seas,
Carried by the solar breeze.
In this cosmic waltz, we find our place,
In the universe's warm embrace.

Sailor's Secrets in the Sunlit Depths

Beneath the waves, ancient lore,
In every tide, a tale of yore.
Sailors whisper to the sea,
Secrets held in mystery.

The sun's embrace on darkened waves,
Guides lost souls in watery graves.
With every breeze, their laughter flows,
Carving paths where knowledge grows.

Leviathans in shadows roam,
Guarding treasures, their hidden home.
Sunlit depths, a world apart,
With currents strong and beating heart.

In coral cities, silence reigns,
As dolphins dance in ocean's chains.
Sailor's songs, in depth they dwell,
Each note a wish, each cadence a spell.

Though the horizon seems to call,
In sunlit depths, we find it all.
A sailor's heart beats wild and free,
Unlocking wonders of the sea.

The Endless Ripple

Whispers in the water's dance,
Kissing pebbles, soft expanse.
Each droplet tells a tale anew,
Flowing gently, dreams pursue.

Reflections play on sunlit waves,
Invisible secrets, the river saves.
A world within, serene and clear,
Nature's voice is all we hear.

Beneath the surface, life unfolds,
The silent stories, countless holds.
Ripples carry echoes wide,
A journey forged, where hearts abide.

In shadows cast by ancient trees,
A symphony sung by evening breeze.
Transcending time, the currents bind,
The endless ripple, love defined.

With every wave, a hope reborn,
Where dreams take flight, and fears are worn.
An infinite circle, beginning and end,
In water's arms, we always mend.

Wings Across Aquatic Heights

Feathers kiss the boundless blue,
Birds in flight, with skies so true.
Over ocean's whispers, they glide,
Graceful arcs, like time they bide.

Amongst the waves that cradle dreams,
The world beneath in sunlight gleams.
Curved horizons beckon them near,
In the dance of air, they persevere.

Above the sea, their shadows play,
In a realm of azure and spray.
Wings outstretched, they chase the light,
Soaring high, hearts take flight.

With every swoop, a tale is spun,
Of freedom found, of battles won.
Unfurling hopes like sails on breeze,
Across aquatic heights, they seize.

In twilight's glow, the flock unites,
Painting paths in golden sights.
In harmony, their spirits soar,
Wings of wonder, forevermore.

Echoing Through Turquoise Skies

Beneath the vast and endless dome,
A melody of clouds feels like home.
With hues of blue and whispers light,
Dreams drift softly, taking flight.

The sun dips low, a fiery glow,
Waves of turquoise, a gentle flow.
Rippling sounds, sweetened with grace,
Nature's breath in this sacred space.

Echoing laughter, the wild winds sing,
Songs of freedom that echoes spring.
Floating thoughts like dandelion seeds,
Carried away where the heart leads.

In radiant moments, forever caught,
The beauty found cannot be bought.
As colors dance across the skies,
The world awakens, the spirit flies.

With every heartbeat, the canvas grows,
Embracing the light of twilight's glow.
Echoes of life linger and play,
Through turquoise skies, they find their way.

Driftwood Dreams

Beside the shore, where tides embrace,
Lies weathered wood, a timeless trace.
Each grain, a story softly told,
Of journeys past and whispers bold.

Carved by waves, in salt and sun,
Driftwood dreams have just begun.
They hold the memories of the sea,
Echoes of what was meant to be.

In moonlight's glow, they sparkle bright,
Imagination takes to flight.
Crafted moments on the sand,
Nature's art, so delicate and grand.

Time and tide, both kind and cruel,
Each piece a gem, a hidden jewel.
In tangled roots or splintered seams,
Lie the essence of our dreams.

Beneath the stars, they softly gleam,
Guiding souls through whispered dreams.
A legacy of waters wide,
Driftwood whispers, where hopes abide.

Soaring through the Amethyst Realm

In twilight's glow, we rise and sway,
With wings of dreams, we drift away.
Through amethyst clouds, we weave and roam,
A journey's end, yet still a home.

Whispers of stars, they guide our flight,
Painting the skies with hints of light.
With every breath, a world unfolds,
In radiant hues, our story told.

The realms unknown, we dare to seek,
In every turn, the mystique speaks.
With hearts aglow, we chase the dawn,
In amethyst seas, we're never gone.

A dance of fate, we twirl and spin,
Embracing the magic that lies within.
So soaring high, we'll touch the skies,
In this vast realm where the spirit flies.

Beneath the Tides of Infinity

Where echoes hum beneath the waves,
In silent whispers, the ocean caves.
With currents strong, our spirits dive,
In deep blue depths, we come alive.

The tides embrace, they pull and sway,
Guiding lost souls along the way.
Beneath the moon's soft, watchful glance,
We dance with dreams in a timeless trance.

Coral gardens, vibrant and grand,
With secrets held in shifting sand.
Among the fishes, we find our heart,
In harmony, we play our part.

The universe sings a lullaby,
As stars adorn the endless sky.
In waters deep, together we flow,
Beneath the tides where the wild things grow.

Starlit Pathways in the Skyscape

Upon a canvas, the starlight gleams,
Crafting paths woven from our dreams.
Each twinkle bright, a call to roam,
In skyscapes vast, we find our home.

With constellations as our guide,
We journey forth, hearts open wide.
Through nebulous fields, we sail away,
On starlit highways, night turns to day.

Galaxies spin in a dance divine,
In whispered stories, our fates entwine.
With every breath, we touch the sky,
In endless wonder, we learn to fly.

The universe holds a map of light,
Leading us onward, through the night.
In starlit pathways, we glide and play,
Creating memories, come what may.

A Dive into the Infinite Aquamarine

In aquamarine depths, we turn and twirl,
Where ocean's magic begins to swirl.
Each bubble rising, a song so sweet,
Pulls us deeper into the beat.

With every wave, the rhythm grows,
A melody of the sea that flows.
We dive through coral, bright and bold,
In shimmering waters, new stories unfold.

The sunlit beams, they dance and play,
Guiding us gently through the brine's ballet.
With fishes weaving in vibrant hue,
In this aquamarine, we find the true.

In endless depths, we shed our fears,
Embracing the silence, the distant cheers.
Through tranquil waters, we drift and glide,
In infinite blue, where our hearts reside.

Shadows of the Wandering Cloud

Softly drifting, shadows play,
Across the hills where children sway.
Beneath the vast and bluest dome,
Clouds like whispers drift far from home.

Each shape a tale, a fleeting thought,
In sunlight's grasp, their form is caught.
A dance of gray, then white, then gold,
In stories of the sky retold.

As evening falls, they lose their way,
In twilight's embrace, they softly lay.
With starlit skies as their retreat,
The wandering dreams of clouds discreet.

A gentle breeze, the night's caress,
Brings murmurs of their soft finesse.
In the silence, we find a thread,
Of journeys where the heart has led.

Through shadows cast and dreams we find,
The wandering cloud reflects the mind.
And in their flight, we see our own,
A tapestry of thoughts unknown.

The Leisurely Drift of Time

Time meanders, slow and free,
Like a river through a tree.
Each moment whispers, soft and light,
In the stillness of the night.

Hours blend as colors fade,
In the twilight, memories laid.
Seconds linger, stretch and splay,
In the warmth of golden ray.

With every tick, a breath we take,
In the dance of give and take.
Life flows gently, ebb and flow,
In the silence, time will grow.

Past and future, hand in hand,
Creating dreams, we understand.
In its leisure, we find our place,
Embracing time's soft, warm embrace.

As days unfurl, like petals spread,
We cherish the paths we tread.
In the drift, we come to see,
The beauty in simplicity.

Notes from an Ocean Song

Waves hum softly, songs of blue,
Carrying tales of journeys true.
Each ripple dances, pure and bright,
In the arms of the moonlight.

Seashells whisper, secrets old,
Echoes of the deep unfold.
A symphony of wind and tide,
Nature's voice, a gentle guide.

Gulls dive low, then rise again,
Chasing dreams, like fleeting rain.
In salty air, we breathe the past,
With every note, the die is cast.

Stars above in velvet night,
Watch the ocean's heart take flight.
In the depths, our sorrows drown,
As melodies of hope resound.

The ocean sings of love and loss,
In its embrace, we count the cost.
Let waves of time wash over me,
I find my peace, my harmony.

Celestial Whispers

Stars awaken, twinkling bright,
Each a wish in the dark of night.
Galaxies spin in silent grace,
In the vastness, we find our place.

Cosmic winds, they softly sigh,
Carrying dreams across the sky.
In the stillness, we feel the pull,
Of a universe, vast and full.

Moonlight dances on the sea,
A night's embrace, wild and free.
In shadows cast by twinkling light,
We seek the truths that shine so bright.

Ancient tales in stardust spun,
From the age of moon and sun.
In celestial whispers, we unite,
With echoes of the cosmic night.

As we gaze upon the above,
We find a thread of endless love.
In the dance of stars, we see,
The beauty of eternity.

Distant Waves of Wonder

On the horizon, whispers play,
A melody of the ocean's sway.
Reflections dance in twilight's glow,
Secrets held where the winds do blow.

Sand beneath my wandering feet,
Time stands still in this retreat.
The stars above begin to gleam,
A tapestry of dreams we seam.

Echoes of a distant call,
In the twilight, I feel so small.
Waves crash softly on the shore,
An ancient song forever more.

The moon ascends, a guiding light,
Illuminating the coming night.
In ocean's arms, we find our place,
Embraced by nature's warm embrace.

So let the tides bring forth their tales,
Of distant lands and whispering gales.
Each ripple carries hopes anew,
In waves of wonder, me and you.

Flight of the Azure Spirits

High above the treetops soar,
Spirits dancing, free to explore.
With wings of light, they weave and glide,
In the azure where dreams abide.

Through gentle currents, they take flight,
Painting the sky with pure delight.
They whisper secrets to the breeze,
In harmony with swaying trees.

With every beat, a heart sets free,
Embracing all eternity.
Beyond the clouds, their laughter sings,
Together on the breath of spring.

In twilight's glow, their shadows wane,
Yet echoes of their joy remain.
Each sunset paints their tales in hue,
Of azure skies that once they knew.

As stars awaken, spirits roam,
In the vastness, they find their home.
A journey endless, bold and true,
The flight of life begins anew.

Beneath the Endless Skies

Beneath the arch of endless blue,
Nature sings her song so true.
Fields of gold invite the day,
Where shadows dance and children play.

Mountains rise to kiss the clouds,
In silent strength, they wear their shrouds.
Whispers carried on the breeze,
Bring tales of love among the trees.

The river flows with gentle grace,
Reflecting dreams in its embrace.
Each ripple carries hopes untold,
In silver threads, their stories fold.

As twilight calls the stars to wake,
The world awaits the paths we take.
With every heartbeat, life unfolds,
Beneath the skies, our dreams behold.

In endless nights and vibrant days,
We find the strength in myriad ways.
Awash in colors, fierce and wide,
Beneath the skies, our hearts confide.

The Tranquil Call of Deep Waters

In quiet depths where silence lies,
Echoes of a soft sigh rise.
The tranquil call of waters deep,
A sacred promise, secrets keep.

Ripples shimmer in the light,
Reflecting stories, soft and bright.
Each wave whispers a lullaby,
Caressing shores with a gentle sigh.

Beneath the surface, life abounds,
In hidden realms, serene sounds.
Coral gardens, vibrant and grand,
In the deep sea, beauty stands.

The moon's embrace, a guiding hand,
Illuminates the ocean's land.
In harmony, all life flows,
A tranquil heart in ebb and glow.

So listen close, let waters speak,
In every current, dreams we seek.
The call of deep, forever near,
A love for nature, pure and clear.

Stardust in the Ocean's Palms

In twilight's glow the waves do dance,
Whispers of secrets in every chance.
Soft sand cradles dreams yet untold,
Waves embrace stardust with hands of gold.

Moonlight spills through the palms' shy sighs,
Each sparkle winks beneath night skies.
Nature's lullaby, so sweet, so clear,
Echoing hearts that hope to draw near.

Footprints linger, washed away with tide,
Memories crafted where feelings reside.
Oceans hold love in their gentle swell,
Stories of lives, each wave a new spell.

In the quiet of night, secrets bloom,
Each breath reflects the ocean's room.
Stars align with the pulse of the sea,
In the palms of night, we're ever free.

Beneath the Celestial Canopy

Under the vast and endless dome,
Where stardust weaves the world we roam.
Dreams take flight on moonlit streams,
Carried gently through crystal beams.

Each star a story, a silent song,
Whispers of ages where we belong.
Galaxies spin in a cosmic embrace,
Guiding lost souls to a warm place.

In the night's cradle, we find our way,
Navigating shadows that dance and sway.
The universe hums its ancient tune,
Beneath the watchful eye of the moon.

As constellations weave their bright trail,
Hearts unite where the spirits sail.
Together we soar, with dreams in tow,
Beneath the heavens, our souls aglow.

Reflections of a Liquid Dream

Ripples shimmer on a tranquil stream,
Mirroring hope in a silvery gleam.
Every surface dances with light,
Echoes of wonder in the soft night.

Floating thoughts like leaves in a flow,
Whispers of magic in the undertow.
A world unfurls in the water's embrace,
Carving our path with its gentle grace.

Upon that canvas, stories unfold,
Tales of the brave and the bold.
Each drop a notion of life's sweet weave,
In liquid dreams, we dare to believe.

A mirror to hearts, our passions ignite,
Reflections of joy, of sorrow, of light.
Through currents we dance, lost in a scheme,
Together we sail, on this liquid dream.

A Breath of Horizon Whispers

While dawn paints the sky with blushing hues,
Fields awaken with fresh morning views.
Each breeze carries tales from afar,
Songs of the morning, beneath the star.

Horizons beckon with arms open wide,
Every whisper, a journey of pride.
Infinite pathways await our tread,
In the dance of life where dreams are bred.

With every step, we breathe in the day,
Drawing in hope as we find our way.
Nature's embrace, a gentle caress,
Fills our spirits with boundless finesse.

A breath of horizon, a sigh of the land,
We wander together, hand in hand.
In each shared moment, in joy or in strife,
We write our stories, the essence of life.

Fragments of an Aquatic Sky

Beneath the waves, whispers softly flow,
Sunlight dazzles, as the currents glow.
Fish dart like thoughts, vivid and bright,
In this realm, colors ignite.

Clouds in the depths, a mosaic's embrace,
Mirroring dreams in this fluid space.
Ripples and echoes weave tales anew,
As the ocean breathes, expansive and true.

Size and shape obey no design,
The essence of freedom in each line.
Stars flicker down through sapphire deep,
Guardians watching while the world sleeps.

Fragments of wonders drift with the tide,
Secrets of the sea, where spirits glide.
Every droplet tells stories of old,
In whispers of silver, adventures unfold.

This aquatic sky, a canvas so wide,
Dances of nature, where mysteries bide.
Fragments of life in a harmonious spin,
Beneath the ocean, new worlds begin.

Charting the Dreamer's Voyage

Sails unfurl on the churning sea,
Visions beckon, wild and free.
Stars map out the paths of old,
Each ripple a story to be told.

Waves of wonder, dreams take flight,
Guided by shadows and flickering light.
An inked horizon stretches ahead,
Where hopes and fears gently tread.

Courage calls from the depths below,
To chart a course through ebb and flow.
In the calm, there lies strength to find,
Words of the heart, forever intertwined.

Whispers of courage weave through the night,
Navigating through darkness, seeking the light.
Every heartbeat echoes the wish of the soul,
Guiding the dreamer toward the goal.

With each swell of the tide, so alive,
The spirit of adventure begins to thrive.
As the journey unfolds, new realms arise,
Charting the dreamer's voyage, the skies.

Celestial Blues at Twilight

Evening drapes a soothing veil,
Whispers of dusk in a tranquil tale.
Stars awaken, tremble, and glow,
In the twilight's warm, soft-flow.

The horizon blushes in colors bold,
Where secrets of night begin to unfold.
Moonlight dances on azure hues,
Painting the sky with celestial blues.

A symphony plays on the edge of dreams,
Flowing like water, where starlight gleams.
Each sigh of the world blends gently with night,
Lost in the magic of fading light.

Clouds drift softly, like thoughts in the head,
Softly they murmur, though barely said.
In these quiet moments, time seems to bend,
Celestial blues where realities blend.

As darkness deepens, soft shadows weave,
In the heart of the night, we learn to believe.
Twilight's embrace, a gentle reprieve,
In the celestial blues, we willingly leave.

Journey Through the Ethereal Waters

Waves crash softly on shores untamed,
Carried by winds, adventures named.
In this voyage where spirits soar,
Ethereal waters declare their lore.

Floating through realms of gossamer dreams,
Life flows in currents, whispers and beams.
Moments of silence, where thoughts intertwine,
A tapestry woven in the grand design.

Ripples of wonder engage the heart,
As horizons beckon, urging to start.
With every stroke, the world unfolds,
Secrets unraveled, a journey bold.

Sunset hues merge with the peaceful night,
Casting reflections in tender light.
Ethereal waters, a path to embrace,
Guide us in grace through time and space.

Together we drift in this vast expanse,
Embracing the waves like a timeless dance.
Journey through tales of love and fate,
In ethereal waters, we navigate.

A Promise of When the Stars Align

In whispered dreams we find our way,
Through cosmic trails, we softly sway.
Hearts entwined in night's embrace,
A promise hung in timeless space.

Dancing lights in the velvet sky,
Guide our souls, both you and I.
With every twinkle, hopes reside,
For when they shine, we'll turn the tide.

The universe, a canvas wide,
Paints the path where love can't hide.
Together we'll chase the gleaming flare,
A promise of love, a cosmic affair.

As constellations light the night,
Our hearts ignite with pure delight.
In every moment, we redefine,
The beauty borne when stars align.

So let us wait, with faith so true,
In endless night, I'll wait for you.
For in the heavens, wide and vast,
A promise blooms, forever cast.

Shadows Cast by Celestial Light

Beneath the moon's soft, silver glow,
Shadows dance, a gentle show.
The night breathes secrets low and clear,
In every flicker, whispers near.

Stars emerge, their brilliance bright,
Casting dreams in the still of night.
With every shimmer, stories flow,
Of distant worlds we yearn to know.

Galaxies swirl in artful grace,
We find our place in this vast space.
Though shadows linger, light will guide,
Through cosmic waves our hearts collide.

Each twinkling star, a tale retold,
In the cool night air, our dreams unfold.
We wander through this endless sight,
Embraced by shadows, kissed by light.

In celestial realms, love takes flight,
Filling our hearts, unbound by night.
The universe sings a soothing rhyme,
While shadows dance, a tale sublime.

The Rhythm of Untamed Waters

Waves crash down with fervent might,
The ocean calls, in wild delight.
Its rhythm pulses, fierce and free,
In every splash, a symphony.

Beneath the surface, secrets dwell,
In depths where ancient echoes swell.
The currents dance, chaotic play,
Telling tales of night and day.

Moonlit paths across the sea,
Illuminate what's meant to be.
With every tide, we rise and fall,
The rhythm sings, a siren's call.

Together we embrace the swell,
In nature's arms, we weave our spell.
With hopes as vast as ocean's shore,
The heartbeat of the waters roars.

In untamed waters, we find our place,
Wrapped in nature's warm embrace.
With every wave, our spirits soar,
United in this dance, forevermore.

A Serenade to the Uncharted

In dreams we wander, spirits bold,
To lands unknown, stories untold.
Each step a note in nature's song,
Together we'll find where we belong.

The mountains rise, high and grand,
Whispering secrets of distant lands.
With every breeze, a new refrain,
A serenade to ease the pain.

Through forests deep, where shadows twine,
We trace the paths where sunbeams shine.
The uncharted calls, a beckoning light,
Filling our hearts with pure delight.

In valleys lush, we pause to breathe,
Amidst the beauty, our souls believe.
With open hearts, we chart our course,
Bound by dreams, an endless source.

So let us sing, as wild hearts do,
In lands untraveled, just me and you.
A serenade to the uncharted,

With every note, love will never part.

The Serene Horizon's Song

Beneath the canopy of twilight glow,
Waves whisper secrets, soft and low.
The sun dips gently, painting the sea,
A tranquil moment, wild and free.

Birds glide gracefully, tracing the air,
A chorus of peace, beyond compare.
Clouds drift lazily, a floating raft,
As time surrenders, a sweet, soft draft.

The horizon blushes, a canvas bright,
As stars awaken, igniting the night.
Cool breezes carry the ocean's song,
In this serene world, we all belong.

Silhouettes of ships in the fading light,
Embrace the calm as day turns to night.
The tranquil waters reflect their grace,
As nature unfolds its warm embrace.

In twilight's cradle, dreams take their flight,
Kisses of starlight scatter the night.
The horizon whispers the tales untold,
In the embrace of night, we grow bold.

Twilight Tides and Starlit Skies

Softly the twilight brings its embrace,
As tides retreat, revealing the space.
Stars like diamonds dot the vast sky,
Whispers of night as the world says goodbye.

The moon, a lantern, bathes all in light,
Guiding lost sailors on their long flight.
Waves ebb and flow, a rhythmic tune,
Dancing in harmony beneath the moon.

Cool breezes kiss the gentle shore,
Nature's lullaby, forevermore.
In the distance, the horizon gleams,
Awakening fragments of lost dreams.

The constellations weave tales of old,
Of heroics, of love, of treasures bold.
Each twinkling star, a wish made true,
In twilight's embrace, our hearts break through.

Together we stand on the soft, warm sand,
With fate entwined, dreaming hand in hand.
As starlit skies cradle the sea,
In this moment, we are truly free.

Reflections in the Oceanic Mirror

The sea, a mirror to the sky's delight,
Reflects the dawn, a spectacle bright.
Gentle waves ripple, a soft caress,
Nature's artistry, we must confess.

Clouds float lazily, painted in hues,
Shades of lavender, pinks, and blues.
Every glance reveals a brand new tale,
As sunlight dances across the pale.

Fishes dart below, with colors that gleam,
Nature's own palette, a vibrant dream.
The ocean whispers, secrets from deep,
In its vastness, we lose and we keep.

Footprints in sand, washed away by the tide,
Echoes of moments when love would abide.
Each wave that breaks speaks of what was lost,
In the ocean's embrace, we pay the cost.

But in reflections, hope starts to grow,
In the oceanic mirror, soft and slow.
The promise of tomorrow shines bright and clear,
As waves of comfort drown out our fear.

A Sojourn Among the Waves

Venturing forth where the sea meets the sky,
A sojourn awaits for the brave and the shy.
Waves call my name with a luring embrace,
As I wander freely, in this endless space.

The sun, a sentinel, watches me play,
As footprints of wonder are washed clean away.
Each crash of the tide sings a sweet song,
In rhythm and rhyme, where I feel I belong.

Seagulls cry out, soaring high up above,
Carrying whispers of tranquil love.
The salty breeze kisses my sun-kissed skin,
In the dance of the waves, my journey begins.

Among the horizons, adventures reside,
In every swell, there's a world to abide.
Mysteries hidden in depths dark and deep,
Awakening wonders that lulls me to sleep.

As I breathe in the salty air so pure,
In the embrace of nature, I find my cure.
This sojourn among the waves I shall keep,
For in the heart of the ocean, my soul leaps.

The Call of Horizon's Edge

A whisper soft upon the breeze,
Where sky and sea meet with ease.
Colors dance in twilight's glow,
As dreams awaken, wild and slow.

Far beyond where the sun sinks low,
An adventure waits, a chance to grow.
Waves of gold and threads of light,
Guide the heart to the endless night.

With every step, the world unfolds,
Stories waiting, yet untold.
Each moment a spark, a daring flight,
Calling forth the brave to ignite.

In the embrace of the vast expanse,
The soul is drawn to the horizon's dance.
Where hope and wonder intertwine,
The call of the edge, forever divine.

Endless skies and waters deep,
In silence, memory starts to seep.
The echoes of the journeys past,
In the heart, they linger, forever cast.

Lifting the Veil of Turquoise Dreams

Beneath the azure, secrets lie,
Whispers of waves, a gentle sigh.
Mirrored depths of tranquil hue,
Where dreams awaken, fresh and new.

The sun caresses, lighting grace,
In every ripple, a familiar face.
A journey woven with threads of fate,
In turquoise tides, our hearts await.

Wandering souls seek solace here,
In a world painted crystal clear.
Lifting the veil, the magic starts,
As we share the depth of our hearts.

With each embrace of the ocean's flow,
A new horizon begins to show.
In the dance of the sea and sky,
Turquoise dreams will never die.

So dive into this watery realm,
Let hopes and fears intertwine and helm.
For in these waves, a life anew,
Awaits in the depths of vibrant blue.

Shadows Cast by Celestial Seas

Under the moon's soft silver sheen,
The shadows dance, serene and keen.
Celestial waters whisper low,
Secrets hidden, tales to bestow.

Stars adorn the midnight sky,
As timeless waves begin to sigh.
In this darkness, worlds collide,
Where every shadow holds a guide.

Sailing through the night's embrace,
We find our truth in the endless space.
Each wave a mystery to explore,
In shadows cast, we seek for more.

Reflections shimmer, dark and light,
In celestial seas, a wondrous sight.
The whispers call from depths below,
As we chase the tides where unknowns flow.

So let your heart be free to roam,
In shadows deep, you'll find a home.
For every star that lights the way,
Leads us closer to dawn's first ray.

Sailing the Ether's Whisper

In silence found within the breeze,
We sail through thoughts like whispering trees.
Ether's call, a soft refrain,
Guiding spirits through joy and pain.

Stars above like dreams set free,
Flowing gently as the heart's decree.
In every breath, a journey starts,
Sailing forth, connecting hearts.

Clouds become our canvas bright,
Painting hopes in morning light.
With open minds, we drift and play,
In gusts of fate, we find our way.

Through swirling winds of chance and fate,
We gather moments, never late.
Chasing visions where dreams reside,
Sailing the ether, side by side.

So lift your sails, let spirits soar,
Embrace the whispers, seek the shore.
For in this dance of ether's song,
We discover where we all belong.

Floating on Serendipity

Drifting where the soft winds play,
A gentle chance guides my way.
Colors of fate swirl and merge,
On waves of dreams, my heart will surge.

Moments dance like autumn leaves,
In a world where wonder weaves.
Each step a whisper, sweet and bright,
Floating onward, pure delight.

Stars above twinkle and shine,
In serendipity, I align.
Paths unknown yet filled with grace,
A smile blooms on every face.

Life's surprises come alive,
In this place, I will thrive.
Embracing all that's new and true,
Floating freely, I pursue.

Every turn brings joy anew,
As hopes and dreams begin to brew.
In the tranquility of fate,
I find my heart where love awaits.

Beyond the Fathomless Blue

Waves crash softly on the shore,
Secrets lie in depths and more.
Beyond the blue where shadows play,
Whispers of the ocean sway.

Gentle tides, a lullaby,
Carrying dreams through the sky.
Fish dart swiftly, bright as gold,
Tales of life, forever told.

Beyond horizons, vast and wide,
Mysteries in the ocean's tide.
Each bubble, each splash contains,
The echoes of forgotten names.

Rays of sunlight kiss the sea,
In this realm, I'm truly free.
Caught in wonder, lost in sight,
Beyond the blue, my spirit takes flight.

Close your eyes and feel the peace,
In the depths, worries cease.
Beyond the fathomless blue,
All of life feels fresh and new.

The Calm Before the Infinite

In silence rests the morning light,
Where shadows fade and dreams take flight.
A pause before the world awakes,
In stillness, magic quietly shakes.

The air is thick with soft embrace,
A moment held in sacred space.
Waves of calm in gentle folds,
The infinite waits, its story unfolds.

Anticipation hangs like dew,
Each breath a chance for something new.
In the hush, the heart will knows,
The calm before all life bestows.

Colors blend in a soft array,
The promise of a brand new day.
As echoes whisper in my ear,
Embracing all that I hold dear.

Hold on tight, the journey's near,
With every heartbeat, feel the cheer.
The moment whispers, embrace it tight,
The calm before the infinite light.

Echoes of the Deep Serenity

In still waters, shadows glide,
Beneath the surface, secrets hide.
Echoes whisper through the night,
In deep serenity, pure delight.

Ripples dance on glassy pools,
Nature's beauty breaks the rules.
Silence sings a soothing song,
In the depths, where dreams belong.

Glimmers of stars in the dark,
Illuminate the world, a spark.
In the echoing calm, I find,
The peace that soothes the weary mind.

Time dissolves in the quiet flow,
As currents pull, and pulses grow.
Every wave, a breath, a sigh,
Echoes of peace that never die.

With open hearts, we drift and roam,
In deep serenity, we find home.
Embracing every gentle plea,
Our souls alive in harmony.

Dance of the Endless Expanse

Under the vast, starry dome,
Whispers of dreams find their home.
Gentle breezes join the sway,
Cool night leads the heart astray.

Footprints fade on silken sand,
Waves recede, a soft command.
Each moment a fleeting chance,
Life unfolds in fluid dance.

Clouds drift by in soft embrace,
A symphony of time and space.
Echoes of laughter fill the air,
In this realm, our burdens rare.

The moon casts silver on the sea,
Guiding souls to be free.
In the stillness, hearts converge,
Together, our spirits surge.

Embrace the night, let it unfold,
Stories waiting to be told.
In the dance of endless light,
We find solace, pure and bright.

Chasing the Azure Mirage

Across the horizon so blue,
Dreamers chase what feels so true.
Rippling waves whisper and sigh,
Beneath the vast, unyielding sky.

Shimmering light, a playful tease,
Fleeting moments blend with ease.
Hearts set sail on tempest seas,
Hoping for the softest breeze.

In the distance, visions gleam,
A world built on hopes and dreams.
Through sand and stone, we tread anew,
Seeking magic in skies so blue.

Waves crash softly on the shore,
Singing songs forevermore.
The journey beckons, we must roam,
In this azure sea, we find our home.

As daylight fades, we chase the light,
With every heartbeat, pure delight.
Together we'll find what we yearn,
In the mirage, our hearts will burn.

Sails Adrift in Serene Skies

Gentle winds caress the sails,
Whispers floating through the trails.
The sun dips low, a golden glow,
As dreams awaken, softly flow.

Birds alight in joyful flight,
Echoes of day turn into night.
Horizons stretch, a canvas vast,
Both future and present, steadfast.

Clouds embrace the seeking heart,
Guiding paths where journeys start.
With every breath, the world expands,
In tranquil seas, fate gently stands.

Reflections dance upon the tide,
Time unravels, no need to hide.
Trust the waves, let spirit ride,
In every heart, the stars confide.

With horizons wide, we will roam,
Finding places called our home.
Sails adrift, yet never lost,
In serene skies, we count the cost.

Secrets of the Cerulean Depths

Beneath the waves, a world unknown,
Secrets whispered, softly grown.
The azure depths, a vast embrace,
Holding tales of time and space.

Creatures glide through coral lace,
In silence, find their sacred place.
Mysteries in every shade,
In this realm, our fears will fade.

Sunlight dances, breaks the gloom,
Painting shadows in the bloom.
Each ebb and flow, a chance to hear,
The ocean's song, both far and near.

Bubbles rise, a fleeting glance,
Holding the essence of each chance.
A world alive with colors bright,
In cerulean, hearts take flight.

As we dive into the vast unknown,
Embrace the secrets yet unshown.
In the depths, life intertwines,
A treasure trove of endless signs.

A Voyage of Endless Echoes

Amidst the waves, the song takes flight,
Whispers of dreams in the moonlit night.
Anchors raised, we sail so free,
Oceans call, a symphony.

Through tranquil tides, our spirits soar,
Guided by stars to a distant shore.
Each ripple sings of tales untold,
In the heart of mysteries, bold.

With sails unfurled, we chase the light,
Every dawn ignites our plight.
The horizon bends, an endless quest,
In this voyage, we find our rest.

A journey woven with threads divine,
In every wave, a love so fine.
Endless echoes of the past,
In our hearts, they ever last.

In twilight's embrace, we find our way,
Guided by dreams that never sway.
A voyage built on hopes and fears,
In the dance of time, we shed our years.

Cascading Shadows of Tranquility

Beneath the trees, where silence sleeps,
Cascading shadows, a secret keeps.
Whispers of leaves, a gentle sigh,
In twilight's glow, where moments lie.

Soft melodies of the evening breeze,
A tranquil spell that puts us at ease.
The world fades, just us and the night,
In the stillness, everything feels right.

Moonlit paths guide our wanderings,
In the night sky, the universe sings.
With every step, the earth does breathe,
A tapestry of dreams we weave.

The stars align, like scattered thoughts,
In this serene space, wisdom is sought.
Cascading time, a gentle flow,
In tranquil depths, our spirits grow.

Under the cloak of the velvet sky,
We find our truths, we rise and fly.
In fleeting shadows, a calm refrain,
In the heart of night, we feel no pain.

The dawn will break, but now we stay,
In shadows wrapped, we drift away.
Cascading echoes of a quiet soul,
In this embrace, we feel so whole.

Horizon's Edge

On the brink of dawn, we stand so still,
Chasing the sunlight, a fervent thrill.
The ocean whispers secrets deep,
In the quiet moments, promises keep.

Where sky meets earth, a line so fine,
The horizon beckons, a mystic sign.
With every wave that touches land,
Dreams are crafted by nature's hand.

Through golden rays, our spirits rise,
In the soft embrace of brightening skies.
At horizon's edge, we dare to seek,
In every heartbeat, our souls speak.

From heights unseen, we take our flight,
In the dance of colors, pure delight.
The world unfolds with each soft breath,
At horizon's edge, we find our path.

With open hearts, we greet the day,
The dawn unfolds, lighting our way.
In every moment, let love extend,
At horizon's edge, our journeys blend.

As the stars retreat, we chase the glow,
With dreams alight, together we grow.
At the horizon's edge, we find what's true,
In the vast expanse, me and you.

A Feathered Touch in the Sea Breeze

Softly gliding, wings in flight,
A feathered touch in morning light.
Over ocean's wave, they dance and play,
In the gentle hush of a brand new day.

With every gust, they drift so free,
In the salty air, a melody.
From shore to sky, their stories weave,
In the whispers of winds, we believe.

Golden rays bathe the tranquil scene,
In their flutter, the world feels serene.
Through azure skies, they take their chance,
In the sea breeze, they sway and prance.

A fleeting moment, beauty's nest,
In nature's arms, we find our rest.
Feathers whisper of journeys vast,
In their flight, we hold on fast.

With every dip, a joy released,
In their passage, our worries ceased.
A feathered touch, a sweet caress,
In the heart of the sea, we find our rest.

As evening falls, they return to roost,
In the fading light, our dreams are produced.
A feathered touch in the twilight's glow,
In the sea breeze, love continues to flow.

www.ingramcontent.com/pod-product-compliance
Ingram Content Group UK Ltd.
Pitfield, Milton Keynes, MK11 3LW, UK
UKHW030908221224
452712UK00007B/790